MEN ARE FROM MARS... I'M FROM MIDDLESBROUGH

Welcome to
MIDDLESBROUGH
The Infant Hercules: fashioned out of the foundaries of Teesside. mined out of the Eston Hills.
Its Party. Party. Party. Everybody round mine for a Parmo !

By Roger McCartney

MEN ARE FROM MARS
I'M FROM MIDDLESBROUGH

Copyright

ISBN 9781520742373

Introduction

Football is not a matter of life or death. It's more important than that like. And so are lasses. In fact, shot us over a Parmo, and I'm proppa buzzin me for the rest of the day, me.

This is a celebration of all things Middlesbrough, the people, the town and the language. It's not about the author being from Boro, it's about the reader being from Boro.

You will proppa laff as you read all about the 'Middlesbruh' male perspective on life and it's chocka with humourous observations and man-secrets.

Owee in and gerrit read canny lad. Ayas coming in or what, you?

Contents

Secret #1: Boro Man is The King of Procrastination.

Procrastination is a concept already familiar to Middlesbrough men; we'll win the Champions League next season, thank you very much!

But it suddenly hit me the other day when I was walking to The Riverside, and I don't mean Wilf Mannion's boot outside the gates like. It was the following thought that hit me: all my life, I have been dogged by procrastination, me like. And I'm going to tell you exactly why this is, some other time.

Indeed, whilst writing this celebration of the Middlesbrough mind-set, I am putting off several other things that I should have already done by now. And Boro too are putting a few things off, like the acquisition of points,

because we should be a lot higher up the league than we presently are like.

Teesside men have a saying: "we'll get three points *next week*". I don't know where this saying came from. I'll afta sort it out later like. Probably from ancient times. Tony Mowbray, maybe. Never do owt today that you can put off until tomorra like. Aye good lad.

Smoggy women are canny at doing several tasks at once. This is called **multitasking**. I read about this in the Evening Gazette like. Smoggy lads, however, are equally as canny at *putting off* several tasks at once. This is known as '**multi-thinking-about-but-not-actually-doing-any-tasking**.'

We will routinely postpone owt until the middle of next week and then postpone it further if there is a League Cup match. Me **laundry** will be done only when we spot our red and white sherts making their own way over to the washing machine. **Bills** will only get paid when the bailiff

personally presents them. If it's good enough for Dicko, its good enough for me.

Me **car** will only be washed once people are starting to write childish messages, with their fingers in the dirt - such as "up the Boro" and "I wish our lass was as dirty as this". Ok, admittedly, I write the messages on the car myself, sometimes like!

Health is the easiest issue to procrastinate over. You know when you get an appointment at the James Cook for six months or even a year's time - that suits me like! I'm proppa head in the sand me. I do so hate to receive bad news of a medical nature. I much prefer to schedule the endoscopy for next year. And then in the Close Season or at worst, an international break.

If the problem is owt to do with 'downstairs', then you can forget it altogether. Funny that - men from Teesside love to wave their genitals about on a boozy night out down the Bongo but ask them for a medical examination of said genitals and they disappear for longer than Gazza after a black'n'.

Our lass, on the other hand, loves a visit to the doctors. I think the fact that the doctor looks like Aitor Karanka may have something to do with her real motivation to visit with such regularity, janoaworrameanlike? She will make an appointment just to discuss colour co-ordination schemes or to announce a new apple crumble recipe, her like.

The reason for Boro male procrastination is simple. We are primarily hunter/gatherers. We love to hunt for and then gather in the three points. In-between hunting and gathering expeditions, we maximise our downtime. Cavemen used to loaf about the cave; we like to loaf about in front of *Goals on Sunday* with Ben and Kammy.

After a hard day's hunting and gathering away at Sunderland, we like to come home to our

caves and be nurtured by our favourite Middlesbrough cavewoman. It's been that way since old mother Cook's little boy, Captain, was a lad. New age Boro man? I'm only just catching up with pre-Riverside Boro man!

One or two things have changed in the last two million years though. We've won a trophy and St Hilda's is being regenerated. Lasses now work, and men occasionally look after bairns. Can you imagine a stay-at-home cave husband back in ancient times looking after the junior smoggies while the *lass* went out and slaughtered a mammoth? Didn't happen like.

Middlesbrough Man should not be castigated for his procrastinating nature. It takes stern resolution and serious prioritisation skills - for us to balance a busy life at home and work and pub - and still be able to fit in eight hours watching Sky Sports.

God willing and more importantly, partner willing, there will still be five minutes left at the end of

the day, after *Match of the Day*, in which to get cosy with our lass, like. This is one appointment we do not wish to defer to a later date!

That is, if your partner hasn't mooched off because you procrastinate so much. Or maybe she's a procrastinator too and keeps *putting off* mooching off until another day.

A lass of mine used to say; "You'll never amount to owt, you, because you procrastinate too much, like"

I used to say, **"ow-way man, let's just wait and see like man pet!"**

Secret #2: It's Just a Myth That Boro Men Think About Women Every Six Sec...

There is a body of experts out there, who we shall for the purposes of this discussion, label 'Teesside lasses' - that think that another body of people – whom we shall loosely call 'Teesside men' – think about lasses n'tha with about the regularity of every six seconds.

The six-second premise was first put forward by someone, probably our lass, a very long time ago, in order to explain why smoggy lads, have the morality code of the lesser-spotted porcupine.

The six-second gambit is an oft-quoted falsehood about the male of the Boro species.

This myth, together with 'all Boro men are canny at DIY', is often, of course, wide of the mark.

There are other myths perpetuated about Boro men, for example, that they all are obsessed with Middlesbrough FC. They are not: some men are obsessed with that other great team on Teesside: Middlesbrough FC reserves. Another myth is that all men talk about when they get with other men is Middlesbrough FC - they don't: they talk about lasses that talk about Middlesbrough FC. Although admittedly in between breaks from talking about Middlesbrough FC.

Of course, the idea that a Boro man thinks naughty thoughts twice during the time it takes Gastón Ramírez

to take a corner is, quite frankly, absurd. Preposterous! Dunner yous know owt about us like? It's a lot more frequent than that canny lass.

Yes, the male of the species is much dirtier than the female. We all know that. Sexual thoughts are omni-present. Why? Because we are men. That is what we do. Sexual thoughts are like Stuani goals, you don't have one for ages and then two come along at once.

The brain is saying, "The next sexual image will be arriving in your mind in a few seconds. Please hold - your continued interest is important to us"

Of course, we think about women every six seconds. Well aye lad! It would be impossible not to. But don't be too down on us, we also think about next week's match every four seconds as well like. Juno, in the time it used to take Juninho to dance past half the opposition defence before slotting it home, we have thought about sex three times and we're pondering next week's tricky away trip to Anfield?

Do not give us any chew about it like. Have pity on us for we know not what we do, us like. We cannot help it. We're men. Let she who is without sin hoy the first stone.

Ouch, away man, watch where you are hoying those clemmies, will you man pet like! Youse lot had berra pack that in like!

Secret #3 Teesside Men Don't Do Platonic, like.

I had a lass as a friend once. I know, weird as. We used to work together and meet up at The Riverside for home games. Our common ground was watching the lads and a mutual interest in getting mildly drunk. And I so wanted to sleep with her.

Which brings me to the Deal or No Deal question and I'm ready to be asked it. Can a Boro guy have a friendship with a Boro lass, without wanting to sleep with her?

The short answer is no, but I fear the longer answer may lead me to further compromise the brotherhood, by revealing yet more official man-secrets.

So, ow-way man, and enjoy the ride, like!

Anyone, who knows the Middlesbrough masculine mind-set – in other words, Boro men - will tell you that we *don't do* platonic. We would like to, but we can't. We haven't got it in us. End of. Simple as.

What we do have in us - is a massive amount of raging testosterone and a burning desire to finish above Newcastle and Sunderland. Oh, and did I mention a primeval desire to mate with every female on the planet? Even those from Pooly. Admittedly, the passing of time and the advent of obesity have tempered this prehistoric urge, but it is still in the mix somewhere. We keep it hidden, but in our minds - everyone is being assessed as a potential sleeping partner. We can't help this thought process.

There are no female friends; just lovers waiting to happen. Boro men, if they're truthful, will agree with this philosophy. If they *don't* admit to it, they may tend to haemorrhage credibility.

Boro women unwittingly put themselves in the frontline, by liking us 'as a friend'. Expect the male side of the partnership to be looking to upgrade his 'friend' status, anytime soon. Friendships with the opposite sex are love affairs in the early stages - hopefully.

Back to the Riverside ladette: She never knew of my aspirations to date her and I certainly never let on, for her boyfriend was a thoroughly nice six-foot ten rugby player from Stockton. She was fascinated with me for my ability to consume two pre match pints, and I was fascinated by her - for her very existence. I used to look longingly into her hazel eyes and watch her ruby lips as she chomped on her bacon & egg fadgie. She, in return, looked imploringly at me, for another white wine spritzer.

She used to bring her friend sometimes, and I so fancied her as well. In fact, come to think of it, I so fancied everyone that came along. I've had many female friends to date, and I've like wanted to sleep with all of them. Sometimes,

male ego being what it is, I'll think I've met *The One* if a woman lets me out in the traffic on Linthorpe Road.

Female match-day companions are *always* better than our same-sex ones because the possibility exists of sleeping with them. With a fellow gadgie, you don't have that exciting option on the horizon. No, it's all about bonding over pints, and conversation that alternates between Negredo's ability and Beyoncé's bottom. All very riveting, but it doesn't pay the bills and it don't satisfy the inherent latent primeval cravings. **Give me Miss Ruby Lips and her bacon & egg fadgie prop any day, like.**

<u>Secret #4:</u> What Boro Fellas Really Think About Rotund Boro Lasses.

This week I have been besieged by Boro-based females demanding to know what Boro men **really** think of their partners, being a touch rotund. Well, one woman from Gresham has politely asked so here goes.

Of course, I could give you a truthful account but as it goes against the man-code to reveal our secrets - if I told you, then I would have to kill you like. However, in the interests of the book, here is the absolute truth, even if my instincts are to say nowt like and scratch my genitals.

To get a quiet life with the minimum amount of chew, like, Teesside men have developed a knee-jerk reaction under questioning about weight issues. If I value having a full set of testicles -

which I so do - and to prevent our lass kicking off like, I will automatically respond in the negative with 'jokin-arn-ya' when asked questions such as "now then, does my bum look big in this, pet?" Diplomatic as, me. Answer owt but negative and there's going to be hell on.

Here's the rub. I am **not** lying, me. **I am telling the truth**, like. If I thought my woman was not fanciable, I wouldn't fancy her. Ergo, I wouldn't be with her. Or more importantly - I wouldn't have got with her in the first place. What more conclusive proof do you need of my sincerity during questioning?

Sure, we would all like to have girlfriends that look like Kim Kardashian. That is a given. In fact, we would all like to have for a girlfriend, Kim Kardashian, but this is just not possible. Just as Santa cannot get around every house in Middlesbrough, neither can Kim.

Besides, this is real world, UK, and just as us Middlesbrough men don't look like Victor Valdes

- the ones that do are keepers, aren't they? - Middlesbrough lasses don't look like Kim Kardashian. Not round our end anyway. And if the lasses in our street did look like her, I would probably be too shy to go up and talk to them. Real women have love handles. Accept the fact. Deal with it. Move on.

I don't expect my women to be perfect in much the same way, as I'm not. My waistline is like Pally Park - it needs continual policing. I also have a boil on my bottom, but we don't need to go there.

Real lasses are not any less desirable than their airbrushed counterparts - and also, they have the elusive quality that Kim does not - they are attainable.

During my observations, several of my acquaintances have gone on about being over-weight, when there was absolutely nowt wrong with them. Trips to the Neptune pool and splodging about at Redcar beach have had to be

aborted or she will turn up looking like Lawrence of Arabia.

Sometimes women will even request, "Don't look at me!" when they take their clothes off. Well how is that going to work then? Am I supposed to move in for a spot of lovemaking by using the handy Braille signposting provided?

It seems to me that Boro women feel they must attain stick insect like qualities. Jokin arn ya? These women look positively underfed. I want to take them home not to have my wicked way but to give them some scran. Under-nourishment is not an attractive quality; you know?

I am not going to lie to you and say that I find obesity attractive. I personally don't although some Boro men do. There is a line. However, curves attract Boro men. **We are programmed to fancy you**. Rounded-tummy or not. I have to be honest and say that the law of diminishing returns will occur after the acceptable level of curviness has been reached. But this level is **way**

beyond what most Boro lasses would think. So, think on!

Secret #5: Boro Man Is Rubbish at DIY. Fact.

Now, it's a fact of life, that men from Teesside are expected to be canny at DIY.

As soon as something goes pear-shaped, or the downstairs toilet pipes begin crying out to have a nice little timber unit fashioned around them, then the man will become firmly fixed in the gaze of expectation. In my experience, this is one of the downsides to having the XY chromosomes.

Tellyerworitisrite, even though Middlesbrough history was fashioned from steel and iron, we are not all craftsmen here on Teesside. In fact, some of us are craftsmanship-challenged but then the table I've just assembled, cack-handedly, back-to-front, kind of gives it away, like.

Of course, our lasses could and should call in the experts, but to allow this would be an admission of failure as a man. The very thought of another fella coming in to do a job when we have enough limbs and fingers, would be the DIY equivalent of being cuckolded like.

The reasons for this expectation of Boro men lie in our caveman roots, when DIY was first invented to ensure survival of the fittest. We sat in our caves, fashioning crude objects out of wood and stone, while the lass prepared roast mammoth for lunch.

Two million years later and things have progressed. Rather than worship the moon, we can now play golf on it. However, I am still sat here attempting to fashion crude objects out of wood and stone. Although modern day DIY is primarily to ensure the amusement of the fattest.

Success at it feeds directly into our self-esteem and, more importantly; feeds directly into the esteem our women have for us. Our qualities as the provider may be under examination. The provider of shelving units, which do not slope, that is.

At school in Dark End, I just didn't get woodwork and metalwork. Sure, I was inventive with excuses, but I wasn't so resourceful when it came to shape the materials into owt remotely discernible. No wonder I used to nick off like. I didn't foresee that one day my life's purpose would come down to the alignment of two holes in the wall.

Because I never listened and haven't since been to Teesside University to get a degree in engineering, my aptitude for DIY is severely restricted and has cursed me all my life. I was 32 before I owned a screwdriver and I was 35 before I used it. My toolbox was stolen once, and I was secretly relieved. Our lass kept quiet because she needed someone to assemble the thirty-two flat packs she ordered from MFI, like.

The only thing that *will* come naturally to me when things start to go wrong will be the expletives. I will swear and cuss like Teesside Tintin. That lad will have nowt on me like, once I've proppa nailed my hand to the table a few times. Indeed, I will be a lot cannier in the creation of profanities than in the creation of furniture.

I will become so irritated, after stabbing my thumb for the third time, that I'll destroy the very object I am trying to construct. This defeats the purpose of DIY, which is to build things, not to demolish them, halfway through the process, once you have part-crucified yourself. And when I drop the hammer on my toe, I will proppa dance and shriek like, with more dexterity than that lad Michael Jackson used to. Then we'll see who's proppa bad, like!

I suppose my ineptitude could be hereditary as I remember that in my childhood our dad allus used to saw into the table and electrocute himself routinely. He used to get proppa radgie as well him like. When they were giving brains out, he thought they said trains and asked for a slow one. Was he daft? A little I suppose; he married me mam.

On Completion of tasks, I will expect much praise and promises of cuddling, later, from her like. Otherwise the next time she asks me to put a picture up I might just answer in the true spirit of DIY and say, **"Do it yourself, our lass!"**

<u>Secret #6:</u> Boro Man Has Difficulty Saying, 'I Love You, Like'.

Boro men are not very emotional like. Apparently. Apart from when we just come back from three goals down on aggregate to win 4-3 in the semi-finals of the UEFA cup. That's a given.

This allegation of our un-emotional-ness arises from our reluctance to say the sentence that can mean so much to a woman - and it is not 'Shall I empty the bin?'

No, the group of words that causes us the greatest consternation and the one I personally have difficulty marshalling to my lips is **'I love you, like'**.

A Middlesbrough man will enthuse "I **love** Marten de Roon: He was fantastic against West Ham and he compliments Forshaw perfectly; De Roon breaks up play and simply plays the ball short allowing Forshaw to dictate play" or 'I **love** McClaren – best manager we ever had'. But ask him to use 'love' in a statement of endearment towards his life-partner and *it becomes a different matter,* as the gadge in the Heineken ad used to say.

'Sorry' is easy to say. I will spray 'sorry' around liberally, all day if necessary. Each time I bump into someone – 'sorry'. Each time I tread on someone's toes – 'sorry'. Each time she says, 'You really hurt me, you' – 'sorry'.

'Sorry' is the catch-all remedy that makes everything better. It is instant verbal healing. "Sorry, we threw away a two-goal lead". In football, when the trainer applies the magic spray to the injured player's leg – that is the aerosol form of 'sorry'.

Just as I reserve the wearing of my League cup winning strip for Sunday best, I will keep back the phrase **'I love you'** for special occasions too.

I will only say it when I am backed into a corner and a proclamation of fondness is the only way out. In partnership-threatening situations, such as an argument, the statement can save the day. If utilised correctly, it can be the injection of adrenaline that an ailing or stagnant relationship needs, like.

Sometimes, I will use the **'love you'** card tactically, like, to get what I want, smooth things over or to put points in the affection bank.

Besides, protocol demands you must sprinkle the phrase into the mix occasionally, otherwise your boyfriend skills may be deemed to be rank. If you are not careful you are then heading for the resultant 'you never say you love me' discussion - and no one wants to go down that road. That may lead on to 'you never express yourself'. At this point, I will be fighting hard the urge to express myself by throttling her, me.

So why are the three words of adoration, so difficult?

Firstly, **'I love you'**, is coming from a place deep down in your heart. By reaching down to find this sentiment, you are opening a duct directly into your soul. Good stuff such as **'I love you'** can come out, but equally bad stuff, such as 'I hate you' can get in. Best to keep the entrance to this channel always blocked by triviality.

Secondly, **'I love you'** is an admission of weakness. It goes against the manly grain. I may as well say 'Please walk all over me - and don't forget to lock up, afterwards!'

As a man, I must be tough, not weak. It's part of the job. I don't do weakness, me. Weakness is not going to protect against the sabre-toothed

tiger when it comes bounding into the cave or nowadays, when the burglar comes creeping into the house, late at night. Perhaps I can persuade him to put the metal piping down by telling him I love *him* n'tha?

The next time your man has fallen short of the regulation thirty expressions of devotion per month, don't berate him - treat him kindly. He's an emotionally stunted cripple for good reason, janoaworramean?

Tell him that *you* love him, like, for as far as the 'I love you' declaration goes - **I think it's cannier to receive than it is to give.**

<u>Secret #7:</u> Why Teesside Men Hate Shopping.

The next relationship I get into; I'm going to find out from the outset if we're shopping-soul mates.

Apart from needing to know if we are suited in the bedroom department, I need to know if we are suited in the department-store department.

If we are going to be spending a good proportion of 'us time' in the Clevo Centre, particularly in the acquisition of new clothes *for her*, it makes sense to find out if we're Cleveland-Centre-compatible. The couple that shops together stays together. Although this is not strictly true as she will no doubt keep mooching off, her like.

My preference is for the SAS style of shopping - get in, get the purchase and get out again in as

quick a time as possible. This renders me practically useless as good female company. If I could I would even hoy in a stun grenade to facilitate the encounter. Ideally, I would be so quick that even the CCTV would not pick me up, which is good, as then I can't be prosecuted for the grenade-throwing incident.

Of course, our lass will out-shop me every time. Even when we are in B & Q, looking at power-saws, she is enjoying the experience more than I am, like.

The only time I genuinely enjoy shopping is when we are in Asda Park End, food shopping. It says on the job-specification of a man that he is the number one provider - so there is a certain amount of role fulfilment to be had for the man, in the attainment of the weekly provisions.

I find clothes shopping a far more irksome task me like. It is a lot quicker and easier watching grass grow - and at least you get to sit down a bit. I don't like owt, apart from Boro Town Hall

Beer Festival, which lasts half a day or more. She is far better to go with her mam, bairn, Roary the Lion or someone, anyone, other than me.

My standing-up span is severely limited, and I will immediately collapse, upon entering a shop, into the nearest chair. You will usually find me in the footwear department not checking out the loafers – but instead - loafing on the chairs provided, watching *Final Score*, if possible.

Buying clothes is like decorating the lounge - it's decoration of the human torso. Embellishment is best left to the lass. Just as I wouldn't contest her selection of sequinned cushions, from Doggy market, I also wouldn't interfere in her choice of frock.

After she's spent an hour trying them all on in *Psyche*, she will breeze out of the shop, saying that nowt suited. I am not so foolish to think that we won't be back before the day is out to pick up the outfit that she secretly liked.

The amount of time I have spent waiting outside changing rooms. You don't get that time back. And if you did get it back, God with his sense of irony would probably allocate you a few more hours in *Dorothy Perkins* or summat like.

Boro women are at home in clothing outlets. Simple as. I suspect they all have that inner catwalk model in them trying to get out, even if the audience consists of only a disgruntled partner and a mirror.

The upside for me is that I get to see her in various stages of dress and undress. And as an unexpected bonus I may get to see other women in various stages of dress and undress as I hang around the changing rooms - legitimately this time like. It's proppa mint that like.

And if I grunt enough encouraging approvals, I might get treated to the treasured *Parmo* afterwards. I'm absolutely clammin' for a *Parmo* me like, after me shopping trip like.

Chicken in breadcrumbs topped with a white béchamel sauce and cheese. **Now that's a pretty canny type of shopping!** ***I'm buzzin me!***

Secret #8: Boro Lasses That Boro Men Like to Avoid

As a card-carrying, red-blooded Middlesbrough fella, I like to meet lasses across a wide spectrum of different types and classes. Providing they are carrying the necessary double x chromosomal pattern then they're in. Simple as. However, there is one type of woman that I like to give a wide berth to, when assessing potential partners. These are, of course, Boro women that delight in copying the behaviour of Boro men: **Ladettes**. Nightmare. I proppa like to avoid them lasses if possible, like.

Ladettes are often more laddish than the lads they are trying to replicate. Only one problem: we don't like it. If we wanted a female companion to be a lad, we would just simply place an ad for a lad. Once women start acting masculine, they neutralise their sexuality, which in turn neutralises their fanciability. The whole attraction of women to us is built upon the assumption that they are just that, WOMEN. Once the lines of gender become blurred you might just as well have a game of snooker with our lass and go to bed with Graham Souness.

Ladettes alarm us because they out-male us. They play football. They like to drink pints, laugh raucously and stub out cigarettes on our hands. They are often better fighters than we are and can out drink us. What's the point in having one for a girlfriend? I'm not having it like. It's like having a date with Joey Barton.

In the bedroom, they also try to out-do us by being more macho and throwing us around the room a little. And that's just the foreplay! Now that's not on! We like to be in charge in the bedroom or at very least be kept informed as to what's happening. I once knew a woman that turned out to be this type. She proppa did my napper in. I met her in the Bongo - and she had fists just like a couple of bongos. If I'd known

what our night of wrestling was going to be like I would have asked her to go gentle with me, as it was my first time with a sexually aggressive woman, me. And last. Hopefully.

In the bedroom, well, it all kicked off in there didn't it? She proceeded to bounce us off the walls and tug us in places I didn't even know were official tugging zones, like. She was asking all the questions like, but I didn't have any of the answers, me. It was awful. Simple as. The next morning, I enquired if she knew the whereabouts of my testicles. On receiving her answer, I collected them from the far-flung corners of the room and fled. I swear down on our mam's life, never again mate.

Anno, it was proppa shocking that like. I was lucky to escape with my life, not to mention my testicles. I am still not sure if she qualified as a ladette or just an out and out nutter. And as I have been proven to be a nutter-magnet, I suppose it could be the latter.

Ayas reading my lips? I'm not having it like. We men don't like women to be more sexually voracious than we are. Voracity is our job. Comes with the turf. We are the Boro men. Lions on our shirts. Call me old-school, but we men will do all the necessary bouncing and tugging, thank you very much! Over-zealousness on the part of the female is guaranteed to kill 99% of all household erections. If I wanted that sort of interaction with a female, I would enter the Claggy Foot mixed sumo-wrestling championships.

In my view, women are supposed to act demurely and flutter their eyelids as they blush at the very mention of the bedroom. Not turn into Ricky Savage on a bad hair day, the moment the bedroom door is locked. That scares me as it would do any red-blooded male and then the only woman **I want then is our mam.**

Secret #9: What Makes Smoggies Cry? Apart from Smog?

Now then, I didn't do sensitivity until I was twenty-one, me like.

Sure, I wept like a bairn when Sevilla stuffed us proppa in the UEFA final, just like any Smoggy. I was proppa devoed me, but the real pain had arrived much earlier - the day the golden-haired girl from our end decided it was over. Then I became sensitive me like.

Growing up, I had always adhered to the 'big boys don't cry' rule. You were not allowed to cry except when Boro got relegated. From the age of five I was expected to be striving towards manhood, and not proppa bawling like a baby. By adulthood, I was an automaton, devoid of feeling altogether. If I so much as showed a nanosecond of emotion, amid my peer group, I would receive the punishment of being jeered to death.

But this new adult pain, initiated by the honey-haired one, was altogether different. The sadness was so great, that the emotion had nowhere else to go other than to explode out through my tear ducts. And I didn't give a monkey's what the peer group thought.

She was the person who first tweaked my crying nerve. In our short time together, we shared a crash course in love. When our love inevitably *did* crash, the lesson became 'how to cry', for she had given us good reason to, her like.

The mourning period for that relationship lasted longer than the relationship itself. Kleenex was looking to sponsor us, and my mates were looking to give us a good kicking, if I didn't shape up. "ayas coming to see the Boro, chore. She's only a lass!" they said.

"You wait, you'll see," I snivelled, and sure enough, one by one, they were all struck down by the heartbreak-virus. Oh well, aggy boo like. It was my turn to gloat and provide the anti-virus - alcohol - and profound slogans - among them the inevitable "She's only a lass!"

Professional counselling could have helped us like, but I embarked on a more immediate remedy - drinking myself silly. Drink only made things worse, and then I really *did* need counselling - for alcohol addiction. I used to ring AA so regularly, the guy, who was getting pulled out of the Swatter's Carr on Linthorpe Road each time to come on the phone, was getting proppa radgie about it. He threatened to give us a coupla bats one munda night I rang him. He went proppa balastic there like.

My decline into cathy-heartedness accelerated as I got older and I have now even been reduced to crying now when *we score a goal* instead of the more traditional tear-inducing conceding of a goal, as you would expect. It's a happy form of

crying like, although to protect the man-status I need to sob as inconspicuously as possible. I will deliver each droplet down my cheek as quietly as possible me like. I was not expecting to sob for England (that's Gazza's job) when I sat down this afternoon in front of the tele for Boro's latest outing.

Although the letting down of the manly guard is regrettable, I find that sobbing in front of a lass can be beneficial too like. It may result in much female nurturing and soothing. Proppa canny that like. As a young'un, a gashed knee would result in the immediate requirement for our mam. Now, I run to our lass, retaining as much macho poise as possible even if tears are streaming.

This interaction is like saying to her, "You take over the reins for a moment whilst I have this mini-breakdown like, and then we'll resume as normal. Aye, good lass!" She may be pleased she's chosen a compassionate human being for a

companion – or riled that she's chosen a cry-baby.

Failing that, and I'm on the phone to our mam.

I don't know why I cry. Maybe it was losing the UEFA cup final in 2006 or the playoffs in 2015. Maybe I'm a bit of a mawk with 'unhappy' stamped on my soul, or maybe I still miss Goldilocks. Maybe I still miss Juninho. She was the one that released the dam that had been waiting to burst; all those years of stubbing my toe, having my virility questioned in the changing rooms, and Boro missing promotion. That was a huge back-catalogue of tears! We Boro men are only human. If you cut us, do we not bleed red and white? **And we are likely to cry as well, us like.**

Secret #10: Question. Do Boro Men Cheat? Answer. Is Dicko a Saint?

The good news is that not all Boro men cheat and Stevie Dixon is a legend by the way. He's sound as a pound that Dicko.

Here on Teesside we are made of steel and iron - we made the world for Christ's sake -and we have lions on our chests. There are some of us do not have either the inclination to cheat or the testicular fortitude. These 'thoroughly nice blokes' make ideal husband material and are known as 'keepers' as basically there is no reason to boot them out.

The bad news is that the rest of the Middlesbrough male population are actively cheating, thinking of cheating or would cheat if an opportunity comes along. The brotherhood

will angrily deny it, but then we claim the right to remain silent in case we incriminate ourselves.

I personally am between cheats now, as you need a primary relationship in order to cheat on it with a secondary one.

So why do Boro men cheat? I'm not going to tell you that it lies in our evolutionary caveman roots. I mean *that* excuse is *so* two million years ago! However, it *is* one of three perfectly valid reasons to explain our propensity to roam.

Firstly, as males, our instinct is to spread our genes around as much as possible. Even as far as Hartlepool. This is how humans have flourished, indeed over-flourished, since our earliest beginnings. You see, if women oversaw initiating procreation, today the Middlesbrough population wouldn't be much bigger than the 25 it was back in 1801.

Back in the day, and we're talking pre-Jack Charlton here, man needed to sow his seed as

much as possible to ensure the survival and advancement of the human race. This means that the need to procreate with more than one partner still resides deep down in our psyche - and doesn't go away, even if we go and lie down in a darkened room. Unfortunately, we are hard-wired to have an eye for the next new partner, even when we are perfectly content with our current one.

Secondly, it doesn't take a lot to make us feel inadequate and that's exactly how we feel when we haven't had enough partners in life. This feeling of sexual inadequacy is nature's way of telling us to sleep about more. Inside every man - even those with geeky-façade - there is a serial womaniser struggling to get out. This womaniser is itching to be let out and once free, will proceed to cruise bars and pull lasses in the time-honoured fashion.

Finally, there is the thrill of the chase. The need to clinch the deal goes with the testosterone filled territory. We are like salesmen, who don't feel they can rest until they've got another signature on the dotted line. Remember Boro men are very much chase-orientated and the thrill derived from it. This drives us on to push up the numbers and hit our self-appointed targets.

Even with these pre-conditions working against us, Boro men can and will stay faithful - unless a certain final condition occurs - that of opportunity. Without it we are nowt. It is written in our chromosomal make-up that we cannot resist a sexual opportunity. Even if you are the offspring of Mother Teresa, you are going to be sorely tempted.

It is not just Boro men that are love-rats either - it's just that we get the headlines in The Evening Gazette. Some of my best women friends have been serial love-ratesses. And worse still, and more worryingly, some have been my partners.

The problem with evolutionary heredity is that it takes so darn long to shake it out of our system, so don't expect any change in man's inclination to be love-rats for the next million years or so. But don't worry, **after that, we may settle down!**

Secret #11: Steel Town Men Don't Do Plaggy.

Football is not a matter of life or death to Boro man. It is more important than that like. And so is cleavage. Maybe not quite as important getting a new Boro top in August each year but it still rates highly on the must-have scale. Or, I should say, the must-view scale. And as you can tell from the fact that we are on permanent ogling standby, we are obsessed by cleavage.

Cleavage is important because it sends an inaudible message to a man saying, 'I am lass' and just as lasses like to accessorise, so do we Boro men. I'm buzzin' me like, when I accessorise with a canny lass on my arm.

My priorities changed, as I got older. When I was a young'un, I longed for a lass with a canny chest. Now I am owlder - I long for a woman with a personality - as well as a canny chest. A

girlfriend once said to us that I never noticed her bust, which I thought was a trifle unfair, as that was the main thing I *had* noticed. There would have been hell on if I had not noticed, I can tell ya kid.

So, with that in mind, you might think if you asked a man if he liked implants it would be like asking a child if he wanted an extra bag of kets. The answer would logically be in the well aye man! True enough, Boro men do like an enormous surgically enhanced bosom, but our fascination is in a sort of freakish sideshow type of way.

Looka, it's a little-known fact, other than in man-cliques, that Boro man will always prefer natural to the surgically improved counterparts. There is something infinitely false and unnatural about implants. Or am I missing the point us like?

Enhancement of the bosom is fine but wanting to attain Katie Price proportions, well that's just

scary, man. I would be afraid, very afraid if I found myself within the same room as that lass and her bosom. For a start, I wouldn't know where to look - as her bust will have taken up the entire available panorama. I mean is there any real need to have a bosom that big? I believe that she and her breasts really are intent on world domination. And if this is the case, I say, "You go lass!"

If Jordan *were* our lass, her chest would obviously give us an inferiority complex like. And, being a Middlesbrough man, I don't do inferiority! Not easily anyway. Well aye, we're made from iron and steel us like. It is not knowledge that is power in the male/female dynamic - it is cleavage. A woman armed with impressive breasts can cause us to act proppa mental like. If I am not careful, I will soon be doing even madder things such as gleefully picking up the tab for a Parmo takeaway.

As one of the thousands of Boro men, masquerading as a Baywatch fan each on Tyne-Tees Saturday teatime, I can vouch that implants can have a certain surface appeal. Pamela's still dining out on her assets even now, or more recently, falling down paralytic on them.

Contrary to female opinion, when I see a woman with implants, my tongue does not roll out like an elasticised red carpet. The official Red Army perspective is this: Cleavage does not have to be Roseberry Topping-like to be desirable. Small is also good. And have I mentioned how underrated middle-sized is? From our point of view, there is no right or wrong with chest-size.

It's all dead canny.

Secret #12: Why Does Boro Man Always Have to Make the First Move?

When it comes to courtship, why is it here on Steel River, that it is always the man that must make the first move? If he doesn't, he may as well de-evolve into a single cell organism, able to replicate with himself. For that is all the attention he will get from the opposite sex him like.

Now that I am firmly back in the dating arena, once again I am cast as the cheetah stalking the gazelle. Proppa predator me like. As I leave my phone number on the car of the pretty woman, I have been admiring for the last few weeks, I feel as though I am the Cheetah me like. The only difference in this scenario to the African bush is that this cheetah wants to take Miss

Gazelle out for a Parmo - not for her to be in the Parmo!

But just for once like, I would like to have a day off from doing predatory. Just for once, I would like to have a go at the gazelle role. Eeee, it would be nice to be on the receiving end of a pursuit for a change like.

I learnt the 'faint heart never won fair lass lesson early in life. But ignoring lass altogether? This is not a successful tactic for the lone male to follow. You might as well sign your own single warrant.

It must be decreed somewhere in the Magna Carta that it is a woman's human right to have males-a-plenty chasing her. The last lass that came after me was when I was eight years old at Park End Primary. She had sweet ponytails and used to pursue me round in an innocent game of playground kiss-chase. Naturally, I was so adept, not to mention proppa fast at running, that I was never caught. As the game preceded my learning to kiss by about five years - thank goodness I escaped! Soon after, the roles reversed, and it became the chasee's turn to become chaser and has been ever since.

Only Boro men that have an uncanny resemblance to Messrs Pitt, Law or Clooney, don't have to sing so hard for their romantic suppers, and generally can expect to scoop up the phone numbers, without effort.

Lasses expect to be courted, simple as, but sometimes, I would prefer to live in a parallel universe – where the lasses chase us like. Then I could flutter my eyelashes and reject advances with the tried and trusted line "No thanks, I'm watching Corra tonight"

Boro men also must attain the necessary balance with our predatory tactics. Come on too strong, too fast and you might scare the bejesus out of her. Too laid back and you will have to go and

join the back of the queue and wait until yon turn comes around again.

One of life's burning questions is why is the aesthetically challenged man going out with the rather more aesthetically blessed woman. It is because he asked. He drew in his belly, pumped himself up and asked. Aye, good lad. Sweet as. Get In. And she said yes, because she didn't have owt better to do this side of the next ice age. All women have downtime in their schedules when no other Boro men are asking. This is when a geek masquerading as Mr Nice Guy can get through. I know - I have got through several geek-force fields during my time on this planet.

If I'd known at the outset it was going to be so difficult to catch a woman, I would have let the pony-tailed one catch *us* a few more times. Maybe I would be a better kisser, as well like.

So come on lasses, spice it up a bit, janoaworramean? **Away and chase us for a change, man pet like!**

Secret #13: Teesside Men Fall in Love More Often Than Kerry Katona.

Swear down like, the first week "I love you" was said to us once. So, after picking myself up off the floor and not wishing to appear rude, I said it right back. After exchanging the mutual love-vow with haste, we then spent the next few years unravelling the commitment, at leisure.

However, such an early pledge remains a predominantly Boro male gambit. It is one of our characteristics, when we go all starry-eyed over a new starlet in our lives; we are unable to hold back. But, at what point is it safe to first tell a lass of your love without scaring the bejesus out of her?

The need to clinch the deal goes with the testosterone filled territory. We are like car

salesmen, who don't feel they can rest until they've got another signature on the dotted line. Remember Boro men are very much chase-orientated us like and the thrill derived from it. Did youse not see us last year in the Championship like?

In the first few days of a burgeoning relationship, there comes a point when it is necessary for the man to clinch the deal. In olden days, we would just club you over the head and point to the nearest cave. Now, because we are a little bit more sophisticated, we may use a mobile phone to text it, but the message remains the same: we like you and want you to move into our cave. Or more likely, can we move into yon clean, tidy cave please?

Pitch this message too soon and the relationship may self-destruct. A premature utterance of 'I love you, like' will cause a woman to run for Eston Hills just as surely as Gordon Strachan coming back to manage the club will.

I once knew a woman, whom I knew was not English as she spoke it far too well. Our first kiss had gone smoothly, and her bruised toe was recovering nicely, from where I had stood on it. Mollies had been exchanged and horizontal relations were on the horizon. The schoolboy error was not, in the note thanking her for a lovely evening - it was in the added PS - that I was falling in love with her.

Naturally, Miss Non-Reciprocal gozzed us out quicker than an undercooked Parmo. When I rang to enquire, a few days later, why she had moved back to Hemlington like, I finally got the answer. "It's because you said you love us like".

Oh, I see! Mental like. Maybe the government can get illegal immigrants to go back home by telling them that **I** have fallen in love with them?

"You never tell a lass you love her n'thaa!" exclaimed my bezzy mate. Whilst, I noted his comments, I couldn't help noticing too, the lack of female companionship. I also queried the colour of the sky in his world.

Obviously, my newly ensconced Hemo-based ex-lover, thought I was some sort of doyle who gets his kicks from falling hopelessly for women after three dates. Well, she was about as spot on as she could get - for I *am* that doyle.

I had acted like a young'un in the game of love - which, being only 42 at the time was understandable. I was only trying to bring her closer, not make her flee Middlesbrough altogether like.

We do delude ourselves though, us like. No matter how much I jolly well force myself - I can't fall in love with someone I met just two days ago. It's that old devil called lust - masquerading as love again.

Sometimes it is good to get 'I love you' out during the first week, meaningless or not. If she walks, then so be it - I hear Hemo is very nice. In fact, to weed out the timewasters, I'm thinking of starting my next relationship with asking **"Hello, pleased to meet you and I love you!"**

Secret #14: Boro Men Can't Be Doing with Home Improvement Like.

It's that time of year again, man - when wallpaper sample books appear, and Smoggy blokes take cover behind the sofa that we will soon be asked to re-position. No, it is not a new series of *Doctor Who* - but time to re-decorate.

The reason for the process is simple. Most couples desire the biggest and best property they can afford. Ideally, they want a palatial residence, but cannot always get one because of restrictions in affluence. It is therefore necessary to achieve the palatial effect in their modest home - by decorating the hell out of it.

Each gender's strengths will be played to in the decoration process. Female brain will be used to conceptualise, whilst male brawn will be utilised during implementation. No doubt, Teesside men

are naturals at DIY. The fashioning of items out of wood, stone and iron appeals directly to our inner caveman, and our Middlesbrough roots. But decorating -should be left to the professionals or failing that - women.

Sure, Boro men can point a drill at the wall and move seemingly insurmountable pieces of furniture, as efficiently as Samson can, but women have ownership of the embellishment skills.

The Female of the species is more deadly than the male - at the arranging of the sequinned cushions, and the placing of the yin/yang ornaments, picked up from Doggy market. Women are, by instinct, nest makers and therefore by extension - nest decorators. It is an innate thing.

Boro men, in their chromosomal make-up, have deficiencies in certain genes that inhibit their decorating ability - particularly the taste gene.

They can recognise colours but are unable to co-ordinate them. They are also deficient in the try-to-look-interested gene. Women, however, have both genes in abundance.

Boro men do not attempt this at home! Put the lava lamp down and move away from the net curtains!

Furnishing is a subject that I have always filed in the mental 'don't-care-about' drawer. I thought *décor* was a type of decaffeinated coffee. And why scatter cushions? Why not just place them sensibly?

In most couples, women are allowed *carte blanche* to furnish. For Health & Safety purposes, it is sensible for a man to interfere or question her about her decorating decisions, only if he is wearing a hard hat. Furthermore, failure to complete tasks assigned to him, satisfactorily, may call his masculinity into question.

Boro men are also shackled by the fact that they lied early in the relationship about their interest in home improvement. Big mistake - the refurbishment genie is out of the bottle and you must now feed the voracious appetite that women have for consistently transforming the dwelling space.

Decorating is like going over the Tranny: once you get over there, you need to come back again and start all over. My view is that it is far better not to start decorating in the first place and live hacky like.

She may seduce you into watching home improvement TV programs, in the hope that you will be inspired. You may well feel inspired - to flee. The will to live will also slowly drain from tha body as a new schedule of tasks is assigned to you.

A good way to make up for the lack of new furniture coming in is to get more creative with

existing furniture, by re-arranging the layout. Careful, Boro man, that it is not ***you*** that is spoiling the ambience of the place - otherwise *you* might be re-positioned - outside the front door.

Her ultimate interior plan may be that '*Chez Nous*', **should become simply, '*Chez Moi*'.**

Secret #15: Boro Man is God's Gift to Romance (At the Start Only).

You must agree that at the start of a relationship, Boro men are god's gift to romance. We will organise a takeaway *Parmo*, buy some flowers from Tesco Slaggy Island and trawl round the gift stalls at Doggy market for matching his and her key rings. Just as any bog-standard lovesick fool would. Whilst I am mooching around, she will do what she does best - transform into the visual equivalent of a million dollars by clarting herself right up proppa like.

At the beginning, it's all about the chase. Therefore, I am romantic. I must be. Faint heart never won fair lass. If I'm not romantic, then it's **22 22 22. Hello is that Boro Taxis? Can I have a taxi for Mac?** You're going home alone, fair lass-less, are kid.

I will initiate the courtship moves, when we slow dance, and she will initiate the moving moves. The first kiss will usually also emanate from the male side. And the first slap from the female side, if the timing is not right.

Evolution has given Boro men the role of pursuers and Boro women traditionally have the role of pursuees. I wish it wasn't the case as I wouldn't mind being pursued for a change, but it's not going to happen. Not unless I join a boyband. And that may be unrealistic; bearing in mind I am no longer a boy.

It is only when the chase is over, and the prize secured that we become romantic dullards. It's like DIY. All the skills are there, but the toolbox doesn't come out very often. We will then only rise to the romantic occasion on Valentine's Day. It is not, as you might suspect that our ardour begins to wane. It is more because our true reserved nature begins to win the battle for internal control.

When it comes to being romantic, we are Jekyll and Hide lovers. We are capable of great love and romance such as on Valentine's Day. Then there is the other side of us where we have been told for centuries to keep a stiff upper lip whilst conquering the globe. This is the everyday partner you see before you today, aka romantic dullard.

It's not that we fall out of love. It's that we feel a fool, for showing love. Even when we were initiating the chase and making all the romantic overtures at the start, we didn't feel right. Sure, we were good at it, but it didn't feel right. We Boro men are naturally reserved. We haven't shaken the Victorian out of us yet. Give us a chance. It's only been a hundred years.

You see inside every bloke there is a swashbuckling, falling-from-a-top-of-the-Tranny-bridge-to-deliver-chocolates-type-of-guy.

Conversely, inside Mr Start-of-Romance there is boring block of stone, waiting to break out and slump down in front of the TV. This version of male will breeze past the flowers stall at Tesco, without giving it a moment's thought.

How do you keep the romance alive? In my experience, women are also Jekyll and Hide lovers, not so much romantically but sexually. Mrs Hide may also tend to hijack the female persona once the first flush is gone. If you can keep tha sexual Dr Jekyll alive i.e. by wearing exotic underwear or summat, then he is more likely to keep his romantic Dr Jekyll to the fore **and buy you flowers from Slaggy Island the next day.**

Secret #16: Are Smoggies Are Up for It? And I Don't Mean the Cup.

It is a question that has haunted mankind since the dawn of time. "Why are we here?" Simple: we are here to push on from last season. We all know that.

"When Is Mogga Coming Back?" is another one. Even though there is to be no more Mogganaut, these two questions pale into insignificance when compared to "should I sleep with someone on a first date?"

Now, as Boro men, we have a certain morality code - that of the lesser-spotted orang-utan. Boro women also have a morality code - that of the greater-spotted orang-utan. You see, it's several notches higher.

If you are used to using a high-morality blocker of say, factor ten, then you are going to block out the attraction rays from the opposite sex altogether. If you want an all over appeal, keep tha morality blocker low, and then some sex will creep through.

But why would you possibly want to sleep with someone on a first date? Three things: chemistry, opportunity and alcohol. It is like the ingredients for fire. Any one ingredient on its own = a damp squib: put them all together and in the right quantities and you're going to get burnt baby!

What to look for: Boro men - look for someone in the Jennifer Anniston mode, preferably in an MFC replica shert. Don't worry if she doesn't look like the goddess that is Jennifer Anniston - just have a few beers. She will slowly start to resemble Jennifer Anniston after a few.

Lasses - if he looks owt remotely like Victor Valdes - then he's a keeper!
Teesside University have come up with a formula to explain the scientific rationale of the chances of sleeping with someone, on the initial meeting. Why? Because it's fashionable.

(Attraction + Chemistry + Opportunity + Alcohol) > Morality of participants = Sex.

If the sum of the first four mood enhancers is greater than the combined morality inhibitors of the two participants, then sex will occur. It is scientifically proven.

Whether he will call you the next day or not is the next in the series of life's burning questions. Perhaps we need another formula, the *Bastard Equation*, to work out if he's likely to call.

If the sex was good, he'll call. If the sex was out of this world, he'll Facebook you within five

minutes. In fact, some of his friends might even Facebook you as well.

Non-returning of calls is not exclusive behaviour of the male sex, either. Many a lad rings a girl the next day only to find he has been given Radio 1's flirt divert number and his soppy message, professing un-dying love, is liable to be read out live to six million people.

Of course, each person has his or her own individual score on the moral-ometer. Zero = morals of alley cat. Ten = routine use of chastity belt. My own score is round about the one/two mark, whereas, most of my dates are around nine. Memo to self: stop arranging dates with women from the South Bank knitting circle.

The chances of making it to bed with someone, first night, are ridiculously low anyway.

Here's my checklist.

1) Is there any attraction shown by her towards us other than the sort of casual interest she would have outside the Raccoon enclosure at Wild Animal Adventures, Stockton?
2) Has she bought the 'I have a PhD in nuclear physics, which I studied in between sessions at the gym' line?
3) Did she laugh when she asked you if you had a police record and you replied "Yes, "Message in a Bottle"
4) You ask her back to yon place and she doesn't call the Cleveland Police like. I'm not in the mood for any chew like.
5) Now she's back at yon place and if you can function at all after all the alcohol you have imbibed, then you're on to a winner.
6) Wait a minute, you didn't realise there was two of them. Oh well, even better.
7) You can't function. Roll over. Go to sleep.

Of course, I'll sleep with someone on a first date, me. It would be rude not to. But due to the vast quantities of alcohol consumed, sleep is all I will do! And I **will** phone her the next day, for I fall in love more often than Kerry Katona, me like. In fact, sometimes I fall in love with Kerry Katona. But that's another story.

So, expect to hear us on radio 1, any day now.

Secret #17: Fat Boro Men Worry About Being Fat Just as Much as Fat Boro Lasses.

My stomach's plans for Teesside domination must be thwarted. Industry no longer dominates the skyline. My stomach does. Doing nowt is not an option. Besides, doing nowt is so last week. It was precisely doing nowt that allowed the paunch to grab a belly-hold.

Now then, lasses **do not** have ownership of the weight control problem. Fat transcends the gender boundaries and men suffer the angst of weight-watching too. For lasses, it traditionally affects the hips whereas in my case it is more tummy centric. My waistline is like Pally Park on a Saturday night - it needs to be continually policed.

I look back with rose-tinted fondness to the Ayresome Park days when I didn't have to wrestle a spare tyre into the budgies each morning. The problem first arrived when I was in my middle-twenties. I woke up one day, and there the beer-belly was – like Steve Dixon, in it for the long haul. Other companions come and go, but it seems that me and my belly is one relationship that really *is* for life.

Sometimes I feel like letting the potbelly win the battle. I feel like saying to it: "OK. You can have me house, me Boro shert, whatever – just leave us alone like."

Sure, I will slim down when there is an important project, for which it is essential to get in shape. Currently, I am engaged in the 'trying-not-to-morph-into-Johnny-Vegas' project. Also, whenever my flab is beginning to hamper the chances of procreation, then it is time for action.

So, why is the belly an initiator of such anxiety amongst us men here on the Tees? It is simply because it is unattractive to the opposite sex. If it wasn't – I'd have two, please! Gerrus one of them Parmos for me like and one for my bezzy mate, the belly, please.

If my figure repulses *me* – and I'm a fan of me - then what chance it will appeal to anyone with the prized double x chromosomes? I wish to attract as many lasses as possible, not just those that are Tele tubby-tolerant.

You know that saying "the past is a place I don't want to live but it's worth visiting now and then"? well I wouldn't mind living there permanently, thank you very much. I was skinny then. I spent the first half of my life as a skinny stick insect. It was mint. If girls approached at Salty beach, it was to kick sand in my face. I was happy as.

Now if lasses approach, it is just to spend time in the shade that my bulk provides. I did

experience a brief window of appearance-acceptability - a couple of distress-free months during the transition from skinny to fat....and then on with the headlong slide into obesity.

Funny how priorities change! When asked at school, what I wanted to be, who could have foretold that a more realistic lifegoal, rather than be centre forward for the Boro, would be to walk to the local shops without getting out of breath.

How dare they build in a mechanism such as getting fat, to stop us gorging our faces off?

I am in self-imposed exile from Morries on the Doggy Town road as the vast selection of cream cakes is simply too alluring. By 2000, my life had spiralled out of control and I was on a 200 grams of chocolate a day habit - even if it was for personal use only.

So, I knocked that on the head like. Apart from me customary seven pints a night like, I have retained only the one other pig out behaviour – the Sunday roast. I devour it with haste, and then I can spend the whole of the following week repenting at leisure.

Another tactic is the wearing of extra-large shirts me like. I figure that no one will realise I'm overweight if I disguise myself as a marquee.

I could try the heartbreak diet. Again, like. The only thing is, I'm out of the loop - so I would need to fall in love, behave badly for three years, get dumped, before the diet could kick in.

But don't worry. I'm pleased to announce the onslaught of plumpness is under control. **My waist is diminishing and my moobs are down to an C cup.**

Secret #18:

Middlesbrough Men are Commitaphobe.

Have you ever had one of those moments? When you walk in a room like a right doyle and lose the plot as to why you're there, janoaworrameanlike?

I lose the bigger picture plot sometimes. I know there is something I've forgotten to do. Then I remember - "Oh, yes. Get married and have junior smoggies."

It dawned on me recently that the purpose of life is *not* to have a good time. It is to procreate and pass on those fiddly little things, genes.

It was last week, as my forty-second birthday bore down on me, that the penny finally dropped. Duh. Hello! Earth calling Roger!

In the past, birthdays resulted in boozy celebrations up the Bongo. Now, I am more likely to embark on a session of binge thinking, about where I went wrong in life. How did Mr Eligible morph into Johnny no-bairns?
I never wanted mini-smoggies - till now. Now that my fathering equipment is a bit battered and probably doesn't work. I've always had a *chaplinesque* approach to fatherhood and had backburnered the whole idea until later in life.

Now I feel like shouting to the world, "Give me a bairn. Oh, and a lass. And see what you can do about saving our steel, will you?" I would love to see a little Roger or Rogella running about.

For years I shunned commitment. Now I embrace it. I welcome it. I feel like saying "owee in, commitment, and sit in my favourite chair by the fire and watch *Match of the Day* with us. And bring all tha child rearing possibilities with you!"

Failure to commit is not always voluntary. A lot of it is 'wrong place, wrong time' syndrome. I cannot even blame it on my own broken-home childhood. We get the point. It was like a Chewsder in Grangetown. It was grim. Move on.

I never found *The One*. It is difficult enough to find *one* at all, let alone *one* with special qualities that would necessitate calling her *The One*.

I thought I had found *The One*. And I had: *The One* that lived around our end in Borough Road. She was like the blonde one in Abba and had roughly the same impact on me as Agnetha Fältskog had on the rest of Europe. She was a cathedral in my life: a massive monument and somewhere to go and worship. It was not so much a match made in heaven as a match made in the Swatter's Carr on Linthorpe Road. Our souls would be interlocked forever. And they were too. Well, for ten months of it. I was happy as.

Unfortunately, she wasn't. I wasn't *The One* for her, but some pasty-faced get from Acklam was. He was soft as shite and twice as claggy him like.

Further auditions for *Wife Idol* were held but all roads leading to marriage turned out to be cul-de-sacs; where you must do one of those awkward U turns to get out. You go all the way down there for naff all like.

That put the mozz on that like. I was like Karanka in the window, I just couldn't clinch the deal. I was far too immature to settle down - I had only just learnt to tie my shoelaces - whilst under the influence - and so I partied like it was 1999.

1999 came. Party over. Boro Taxi for McCartney. All the guests had gone home or got married. Just as I was envisaging a *Last of the Summer Wine* future with my two bezzy mates - they got married. No, not to each other, doyle!

I was always the best gadge and never the groom. One day, Forty came up and gave me a coupla bats on the shoulder. I politely requested 'can I not cadge another twenty years of prime time' but Forty replied 'yaravinalaffarnya!'

So, you see the Middlesbrough dock clock tower is ticking. Sitting on the shelf is no longer an option. I am still looking for *The One*. The nearest I've got so far is watching *The One Show*. But there is still time. Time is what we *do* have. A willing bairn-machine is what we *don't* have. But I'm working on it.

So, what are the chances of our mam turning into our nanna any time soon? **As a great Middlesbrough man used to say: "Not a Lot."**

Printed in Great Britain
by Amazon

53560712R00054